I SURVIVED THYR
RELATIOI ___ DIDN'T

I SURVIVED THYROID CANCER, BUT MY RELATIONSHIP DIDN'T

What I Wish I Had Known

JANELLE SINCLAIR AUSTIN

ISBN   978-1-7314-5773-8

To All Thyroid Cancer Warriors,

It is only when we are forced into the darkness, at our most naked and vulnerable selves, true strength and courage can emerge.

Contents

Acknowledgments

Kelly, you gave true love and support in a most difficult situation. We were only given but a brief moment in time; there are no words. May you have your true happiness.

To my family and friends, too many to name, that believed in me and supported me through my toughest times. I am truly blessed to have you all in my life.

Charlene, I greatly appreciate your taking the time to read my manuscript and give your personal and professional advice. You were right, I did have more to say!

Darlene, thank you for your unending generosity and talent to get the right photo.

Leanne, thank you for your open and heartfelt post and for your trust in me to share it.

INTRODUCTION

Take a look at my pill. This tiny little blue pill that I take every day, as soon as I wake, with my full glass of water, faithfully. This tiny little blue pill is life in a bottle for me, my thyroidless self. It is what my body needs to function without my God given thyroid which was cancer ridden. Without my pill, I will die. Sounds like a great pill, right? Well, there's more.

This tiny blue pill also puts me into an induced hyperthyroid state. A state in which anxiety runs rampant, tears flow more freely than ever before, rage comes quickly when things don't fall into place, and fatigue is unending. My heart races, my brain never turns off, I'm exhausted yet can't sleep, I have no desire for intimacy with my husband, and I lash out at my kids and don't even know why. I try to verbalize my feelings but always sound like I'm looking for excuses. I miss the person I once was.

You see, I take this pill to live. We can replace an organ with a pill. Carry on as if everything remains the same. To

those who have their own thyroid, I tell them be thankful. There are no words to make them understand. For those in my same boat, you are my people. You all get it and for that, I'm thankful.

Cheers to my pill popping friends!
Side note, I'm not having a mental breakdown, just a shitty day and just need to know that someone else understands.

-Leanne Gauger Knapp

A NOTE FROM THE AUTHOR

Cancer. No one believes it will happen to them. That is what we tell ourselves so as to not think about our own mortality.

My original intent to write this book was to help others be more proactive at the start of their cancer journey as I had experienced a medical misdiagnosis during the time of my first surgery that was preventable. But then, seemingly overnight, I lost my drive, my focus. I would sit down to write, and I wasn't able to put two sentences together. My mind was filled with thoughts but nothing I could make sense of. I couldn't concentrate. I lost interest. I shelved the book idea.

I spent the next two years trying to return to my life *pre-cancer*, but my plan would prove to be futile as I had no clue the emotional and mental impact I was facing *post cancer*. It took the most devastating thing to happen; more devastating than being told I had cancer, to force me to realize I wasn't *me* anymore and help find my way back. Thus, giving me the drive again to write this book.

My hope for sharing my story is to help other cancer patients and their loved ones. It is most important to think of them, as they are suffering too. If I had known what I would be up against during my cancer journey I may have been able to have had a different outcome both personally and health wise.

I've written this as accurately as possible. Piecing together events after my first surgery was a jigsaw puzzle at times. I referenced to check registers, medical documentation and my mom's memory. My treatment had more of an effect on my memory than I realize, even at the very moments I am writing this.

The names of my doctors and my ex-partner have been changed for their privacy.

PROLOGUE

The thyroid, an endocrine gland located in the base of the neck, produces hormones. It is also known as the butterfly gland due to the shape. The two main hormones the thyroid produces are triiodothyronine (T3) and thyroxine (T4). These hormones are made from the iodine in foods we eat.

T3 and T4 primarily regulate metabolism, heart function, digestive system, brain function, including mood, muscles and bones. These hormones are also associated in function of sex hormones, insulin and cortisol. Thyroid produces mostly T4 which is inactive until multiple tissues, organs and mainly the liver convert it to T3, the active form which is required to interact with cells.

The pituitary and hypothalamus glands in the brain regulate the thyroid and tell it when to release T3 and T4. The hypothalamus produces thyrotropin-releasing hormone (TRH) that alerts the pituitary to release thyroid-stimulating hormone (TSH) to signal the thyroid to make more, or less, of T3 and T4.

Thyroid hormones are major players in keeping the body healthy physically, emotionally and mentally. So, when we thyroid cancer patients are told upon diagnosis "You have the *good* cancer," doctors are committing an injustice to patients. Many people living without a thyroid after cancer, are in a constant battle to return to the way they felt before their thyroid was removed. A thyroid hormone pill can never replace an actual gland in the body. It will keep us alive and functioning, but usually at a cost no one, but a thyroid patient, can truly understand.

ONE

The Beginning of the End

Sometime in 1999

I was enjoying an evening with a couple I was close with, my friends Rhonda and Christie. They were friends I could count on, friends that I had a lot of laughs with and enjoyed in depth conversation at times. That night Rhonda proposed a hypothetical question to me. "If you were in a relationship with someone and they were diagnosed with a serious illness would you leave the relationship?" My response was an immediate "No." They both agreed with my answer. Rhonda said they had proposed the same question to other friends and some family and to their surprise some people admitted that they would have no problem leaving the relationship; that they wouldn't want the *burden* of having to care for someone.

Little did we know at the time how that conversation would later come into reality for each one of us. Rhonda was soon diagnosed with cervical cancer. She went through surgeries, chemotherapy and radiation.

She even traveled to Mexico for experimental treatment. She fought for her life as a true cancer warrior would. Christie was by her side through everything. Sadly, Rhonda's cancer metastasized, and she eventually went on hospice. Christie cared for Rhonda in their home until she passed in November of 2002.

A couple years later as Christie was settling into a new relationship she was diagnosed with chronic lymphocytic leukemia. After watching Rhonda follow all the traditional treatment protocols of chemotherapy and radiation and not get better, Christie announced she only wanted to do holistic treatments. I remember this being a huge source of contention with her family and her new partner. Everyone was afraid she was basing her decisions on her emotions rather than with her common sense. Christie eventually relented and did chemotherapy but also incorporated significant health lifestyle changes along with it. Christie did go into remission after treatment, but her partner ended up leaving the relationship. I'm sure the stress from the cancer was a big factor.

Neither the person with the disease nor their partner really know the toll it will take on them at the initial phase of the diagnosis, during treatment, and afterward, when both are trying to maintain the relationship they had originally. It was my turn next.

August 2015

Christie was losing the battle with her leukemia. She had been in remission for several years until it came back and metastasized to her brain. Her oncologist gave her up to one month to live. Christie wanted to pass away at home with hospice. Family and friends committed to taking care of Christie around the clock until she was gone. It was a surreal time. Less than a year before she was going through chemotherapy again and hoping to kick cancer's butt a second time.

Kelly, a close friend of Christie and someone I had dated seventeen years earlier, flew in from out of state to say goodbye to our friend. Kelly and I spent the night taking care of Christie together. It was evident she wasn't going to make it much longer; she was in such pain. It was hard to watch my friend suffer.

The next night we went back to take care of Christie, she passed away surrounded by friends and family. She was one of the truest friends I've ever known, and I feel blessed to have had her as a close friend the short time I did.

It was an emotional time. Old feelings were being stirred. I had always felt Kelly was *the one that got away.* Kelly and I had stayed in touch here and there over the years and there was always a dance around how we still felt about each other. We quickly realized we wanted to be together again. I had a dichotomy of feelings. I was sad for losing Christie but happy for reconnecting with Kelly. I felt that I had the love of my life back and nothing could ever tear us apart again, or so I thought.

Fall 2015

A few weeks after Christie passed Kelly flew back to attend her memorial service. We spent the next several days celebrating our friend and reconnecting with each other. We both felt that Christie had a hand in bringing us back together.

A month later Kelly came back to celebrate her birthday with me. We had dinner with friends then headed to Seattle for a football game. Being with Kelly again I felt my life was complete, like I was finally home. Kelly flew back home to Nevada and we continued our long-distance relationship over the phone while Kelly looked for jobs in Washington, closer to me.

Late October I went to see my medical provider for a routine visit. While palpating my neck she found a lump on the right side. It was nothing too significant but a definite difference than the left side. She ordered blood work and a thyroid ultrasound. I felt fine and she didn't act overly anxious, so I wasn't overly concerned. Being a registered nurse should have made me more cautious of my own health but for some reason I wasn't worried. I never thought I would have to face a serious illness. That only happens to other people...

The next week at work I mentioned my medical appointment to the physician I worked for, an ear, nose and throat physician (ENT). He palpated my neck and agreed that there was a definite lump that shouldn't be there. I looked at my neck in one of our exam rooms and only a slight difference was noticeable, but I could now see it. I had my blood drawn and it didn't show any abnormalities with my TSH, thyroid stimulating hormone level. I then had the thyroid ultrasound which did show a 3.6 cm mass on the right thyroid lobe. Characteristics of the mass were described as having internal vascularity and microcalcifications. An FNA, fine needle aspiration, was recommended by the radiologist reviewing the ultrasound, as these were characteristics of malignancy. I scheduled the FNA and looked to my boss for guidance. Although he was an ENT he did not specialize in thyroid disorders. He recommended I consult with a newly graduated ENT physician in town who did specialize in thyroid.

TWO

Hindsight is 20/20

November 2015

I met with the new ENT, Dr. Smith, prior to my FNA. Dr. Smith was young, confident and a bit on the cocky side. He told me that I probably did not have thyroid cancer but if I did it was nothing to worry about. Dr. Smith said if I was to have cancer that "Thyroid cancer is the best cancer to get." Really? I thought to myself. I was under the general belief that any cancer was not good. Being the patient, I sat there quietly as Dr. Smith explained if the mass was cancerous the recommendation would be to remove my entire thyroid. I was certainly hesitant because who wants an entire body part removed? This wasn't my diseased appendix that served no purpose to my well-being, this was a gland that serves many purposes. He stated with my thyroid removed I would just take a thyroid hormone replacement pill every day and go on to live a normal life.

I don't know if it was how sure of himself, he was or the fact I was even having a conversation of possibly having cancer, but I didn't question Dr. Smith. I had read comments online from thyroid cancer patients who warned against doctors with nonchalant attitudes when it came to thyroid cancer, but unfortunately, I did not heed their advice.

The appointment lasted fifteen minutes and I was out the door. I called Kelly to go over the visit with Dr. Smith. She was supportive of what I was feeling and facing in the future. I never did ask how she felt about it.

I recall years working alongside with my physician whenever he had to discuss a cancer diagnosis with a patient. It was always done with seriousness of what they were facing but also with kindness and compassion. All too often thyroid cancer patients aren't taken seriously as true cancer patients. I can't stress enough if a doctor doesn't treat your health with the utmost importance as any other person or diagnosis, fire them and find one that does. Cancer is cancer.

The next week I went in for my FNA. It was an ultrasound guided FNA meaning the doctor, a radiologist, would insert a very fine needle into the mass on my thyroid to collect cells to determine if they were malignant. Ultrasound guided means the radiologist would use the image of my thyroid on the monitor to make sure the needle was inserted where it needed to be in the mass itself. I was numbed at the aspiration site. The radiologist collected a few samples and it was over. The whole procedure took around thirty minutes. I didn't experience too much pain during the collection but for several days following the biopsy my neck muscle was incredibly sore.

I received the results of the FNA the next day. I had told the radiologist I was a nurse and the physician I worked for, so I think he rushed my results as a professional courtesy. The pathology showed papillary carcinoma. Papillary carcinoma is the most common and slowest growing of the four types of thyroid carcinomas and like any other cancer, it can spread to the lymph nodes, lung, brain or bones if it is advanced. Although I'm a nurse, I became a patient the moment I was diagnosed with cancer. I may have been in disbelief or I may have been in shock, but I didn't take the initiative to thoroughly research my own diagnosis. I relied solely on Dr. Smith's so-called expertise. This was a mistake.

I immediately contacted Dr. Smith's office after receiving my pathology results. I had his medical assistant schedule my surgery for two weeks out, the day after Thanksgiving. It was the soonest I could get in and I wanted the cancer out as soon as possible. I called Kelly and she made plans to drive up to be with me for my surgery.

We spent an incredible Thanksgiving together with my family. They were just as taken with Kelly as I was. I felt like the luckiest person in the world, even despite my cancer diagnosis. I was on an emotional high.

The following morning, I checked in for surgery and waited. Dr. Smith was running behind, so I had more time to anticipate what was coming. Kelly sat with me as my boss and my family popped in and out to wish me well. I had been through a lot of surgeries throughout my forty-five years; I had multiple ear surgeries, appendectomy, hernioplasty and a couple cosmetic procedures. I knew this surgery held precedence over all the others although I didn't let it show.

Dr. Smith told Kelly and my parents that the surgery went well. He removed my entire thyroid and two surface lymph nodes he saw during the procedure, one from the left and one from the right. It is common for the surgeon to recommend an overnight stay in the hospital after thyroidectomy. Complications can range from swelling to blood calcium levels dropping if the parathyroid glands are accidently removed along with the thyroid. I had convinced Dr. Smith at my consult appointment that I didn't want to stay overnight following surgery. Being a nurse and having Kelly with me to watch for any complications, Dr. Smith agreed I could plan on going home. Usually I have a hard time waking up after anesthesia and this time was no different. Kelly told me the nurses tried several times to rouse me and I wasn't flinching at all. As soon as the nurse threatened to keep me overnight my eyes flew open and I told her I was going home. That did the trick. I learned much later from a psychologist and an integrative medicine nurse practitioner, that general

13

anesthesia can have a lasting effect on our brain function up to a year after being put under. I sure wish I would have known this prior to this surgery and the ones to follow. It would have helped explain a lot.

The day following my thyroidectomy I started on calcium, in case the parathyroid glands were affected, and a common synthetic thyroid replacement medicine. Kelly made oatmeal for breakfast, something that should have been easy to eat. The pain from trying to swallow was not something I expected but totally understandable considering the trauma and swelling from surgery. With each passing day I felt better and better. Kelly was a great caregiver making sure I had everything I needed. Within a week I returned to work and felt fine to do so.

December 2015

I met with Dr. Smith a week after surgery for my post-operative appointment. He told me the next step would be to meet with an endocrinologist who would monitor my thyroid hormone levels as I would be on replacement therapy for the rest of my life. *Hmmm, go on to live a normal life huh?* I would also be prepared for RAI, radioactive iodine therapy, to kill any remaining thyroid cancer cells.

I was curious, since Dr. Smith recommended I have my left lobe removed along with my right lobe, if any cancer was found in the left. He said "No, just the right side as well as the lymph node." I was kind of disappointed in that very moment that I had agreed to have my whole thyroid taken, but it was nothing I could take back. The medical assistant set my appointment with the endocrinologist, Dr. Jones. I thanked Dr. Smith and left my appointment. As I got in my car I glanced at my copy of the pathology report. It did, in fact, state a single, tiny foci located in the left thyroid lobe. So, abnormal cells were present. It soothed me a little knowing the decision for the total thyroidectomy was the right one.

I met with Dr. Jones a couple weeks later. She recommended another ultrasound prior to the RAI since I had a positive lymph node removed. She explained that RAI does not kill bulk, i.e. a cancerous lymph node. It only kills microscopic traces of cancer. I scheduled the ultrasound after the first of the new year and planned to follow up with Dr. Jones once we had the results.

Meanwhile I flew to Nevada to spend New Year's Eve with Kelly. I remember the fireworks going off as the plane was descending into the airport. My health was a fleeting blip in my mind as feelings of an awesome future with the love of my life filled my heart. We spent an amazing few days together. We talked about the future and planned on getting married after I was over my cancer hurdle. Kelly shared with me she had never wanted to be married until I had come back into her life. The morning we got into her car to take me back to the airport, Kelly cried uncontrollably because I was leaving. I knew at that moment how much I was truly loved. It is a feeling like no other.

THREE

Here We Go Again

January 2016

I returned home and had my neck ultrasound on January 4th. Dr. Jones called me with the results a few days later. The ultrasound showed one lymph node of concern on the right, the same side the cancer was on from the other node and the tumor on the thyroid. Dr. Jones suggested I could follow up with Dr. Smith to remove the node or we could "watch and wait."

When I shared the news with my mom she wanted me to consider getting a second opinion in Seattle. Her husband had undergone cancer treatment years earlier in Seattle for mantle cell lymphoma and she knew they had top cancer doctors there. My dad had also recently seen one of the top head and neck surgeons in Seattle for a base of tongue mass that ended up being benign. I agreed a second opinion was wise considering I was dealing with something so serious. Kelly was supportive of whatever I wanted to do. I really could not have asked

17

for a more caring partner. I scheduled an appointment with my dad's surgeon, Dr. Baugh.

Within a week my mom and I were sitting in Dr. Baugh's office in Seattle going over my thyroid cancer story. The many awards voting him one of Seattle's top head and neck cancer surgeons by his peers, that lined his exam room wall, assured me I was in the right hands. Dr. Baugh was young, tall and very personable. His worn cowboy boots gave him away as being a down to earth guy. He was also serious about what I was facing. He asked to see my CT scan. I told him I had not had a CT, only 2 ultrasounds, one thyroid and one neck. He looked a bit perplexed as he wondered why I hadn't had a neck CT done given my cancerous node that was removed. A CT scan, also known as computed tomography scan, uses computer processing to produce cross sectional images of the scanned area. CT scans show more detail than an ultrasound, especially when done with contrast dye which is injected through an IV. The contrast highlights any abnormalities as it is iodine based and the x ray imaging cannot pass through the iodine, causing the image to stand out more. Ultrasound imaging uses high frequency sound waves to make an image instead of radiation.

Since we already knew about the one suspicious lymph node from the last ultrasound Dr. Baugh suggested we go ahead and schedule a radical neck dissection, as he was confident I had more than one suspicious node. He had me do a neck CT with contrast before I left the office. He wanted to see exactly what he was going in after.

Two weeks later I was in Seattle with Kelly and my mom for my second cancer surgery. I wasn't feeling scared, just anxious to get it over with. I knew with Kelly by my side I could get through anything life threw at me. After spending the evening downtown, Kelly and I were back at the hotel turning in for the night. One minute I felt fine and the next minute I felt an overwhelming sense to cry. Kelly tried to console me, but I wasn't able to get my emotions out; everything I was feeling just seized up immediately. It was at that moment I wish I could have started paying attention to my abnormal emotional state.

The morning of my surgery we all met with Dr. Baugh. He was in green surgical scrubs and his worn cowboy boots. He explained my CT showed several more affected lymph nodes than just the one from the ultrasound. He was confident he could go in and strip out the ones that were diseased. As the surgical team prepared me for the operating room, each one of them couldn't speak highly enough of Dr. Baugh's expertise and assured me I had one of the best surgeons in Seattle. My mom and Kelly were doing their best to support me. As I look back I can only imagine the stress and worry they were under as well. I don't think I ever asked them how they were feeling at the time. After all, I was the cancer patient. Wasn't it all supposed to be about me?

Dr. Baugh removed twenty-one lymph nodes during my neck dissection. At the time I thought it was a lot, but I've learned some thyroid cancer patients can have over a hundred removed. The surgery went well, and I was sent to a hospital room after recovery to make sure I was alright before I left for the hotel. I had expressed the same preference with Dr. Baugh regarding not wanting to stay overnight in the hospital. Our hotel was connected to the hospital, so Dr. Baugh felt alright to let me go back to my room since I was close enough if any complications arose. I did have a drain stitched in my neck to collect fluid until the next morning; this would prevent any pockets of fluid from building up under my incision.

As I was sitting in my hospital room waiting for my dinner I felt a nagging irritability. It was different from being *hangry* (angry from being hungry). My mom said something that rubbed me the wrong way and I shot back at her with a mean remark. Although I can't recall exactly what was said, I do remember feeling ashamed that I was mean, but I couldn't help it, I had no filter.

The next morning Kelly ordered room service and we invited my mom to come to our room to eat with us. We were running a bit behind as I had an appointment to get my drain removed. Again, my mom said something that rubbed me wrong and I snapped at her. I assume because of the situation my mom didn't acknowledge my bad behavior. Why was I being so mean? My mom was only trying to be supportive. We ate our breakfast and headed to my appointment.

Soon we were on the road home. Kelly was driving my car and my mom rode in the backseat. The car was full of luggage and packages. My mom had packed everything including the kitchen sink it seemed. Aside from the freeway noise I kept hearing a rubbing sound. My mom and Kelly didn't notice so I tried to ignore it, but it was grating on my nerves. I asked Kelly to pull over. So here I am, a surgical patient with a fresh neck incision, on a mountain pass, in ankle deep snow, inspecting my car. It appeared one of the rear wheel wells was lower and the trim was rubbing on the tire. I opened the trunk. It was packed full, with luggage and shopping bags from three women, but no kitchen sink. My irritability kicked into high gear as I was throwing and shifting luggage to take the weight off. I must have looked like a mad woman to my mom and Kelly, although they said nothing.

Back at home that night I was preparing a bath. A text came up on my phone from a person in my past. It was a relationship that had not been emotionally healthy for me. The text was out of concern about my cancer. I didn't think much about it either way, but Kelly didn't like it and didn't think I should respond. I felt like I should be polite and respond and that Kelly was being over protective. I knew how far beyond my past relationship I was. I was in a new place with Kelly and was never so sure of what I wanted for my future. I responded back to the text the next day with a thank you and didn't think about it again.

I woke up the next morning and noticed that my right eye felt strange. I looked in the mirror. My right eyelid was droopy. I immediately called Dr. Baugh's office and was told most likely it was Horner's syndrome. This is a rare complication from neck surgery where the nerves can get damaged. I was told it may or may not resolve. I must admit, at that point I was starting to wonder what other bad luck was coming my way next.

I spent the next several days recovering. Kelly was used to being up early due to a morning coffee addiction but was always respectful to let me sleep late. Most days I think I slept up to twelve hours. Even though I got plenty of sleep I would roll out of bed and feel immediately irritated. I was already a different person.

Kelly would later tell me "I thought you just didn't like me anymore." It broke my heart to hear that. Kelly flew back home, and I awaited my next hurdle.

I did consult with an ophthalmologist from the practice I worked for and was assured the problem with my droopy eyelid could be surgically repaired. But the Horner's eventually resolved itself. I had been taking a curcumin supplement which has anti-inflammatory and anti-cancer properties. I was also taking an organic mushroom supplement Kelly was sending me. Whether the Horner's resolved on its own or had help from the supplements I don't know, but it was never an issue again.

A week after my neck dissection I received a call from a colleague of Dr. Baugh, involved in my case. She told me that out of the 21 lymph nodes removed that 16 were positive for cancer. The tumor board met to discuss my case and decided my RAI should be 160mCi, which is a high dose, but appropriate given the extent of my cancer. They would contact Dr. Jones with their recommendation.

I also received a call from Dr. Smith within a few days after hearing from Dr. Baugh's colleague. He had received the news of my new diagnosis. He mostly stumbled through the brief conversation, "Uh yea, I got the results of your surgery. So, you had more in there, huh, uh, uh…" I was polite to him but short. At that point I wasn't too impressed, having to had endure a second surgery because Dr. Smith wasn't thorough with my care. Also having to take more time off work and another eight thousand dollars out of my pocket on top of what I already paid for my previous surgery not 2 months earlier. I was not happy. So much so, that I let this provide a huge source of stress and anger that I carried for over two years. I made several attempts over a ten-month period to seek answers with Dr. Smith's employer before paying off the remaining seven hundred dollars they wanted for my first surgery. I was ignored over and over despite my pleas for answers. I finally received a letter from his employer's, Quality of Care group, stating that Dr. Smith and his employer had met my standard of care. Um, no, you didn't actually… I was later given the name of a high-profile malpractice attorney out of Seattle, but ultimately, I decided that the stress and negativity of a lawsuit could be more detrimental to my overall health, so I decided to call it a learning experience and move on. Although I do share my story with others and strongly encourage second opinions.

FOUR

I've Changed

February 2016

Back at work I was trying to get back on track resuming my normal routine. But I was stumbling a bit. As a nurse I must stay sharp and on task. Vulnerable people are dependent on it. One morning while getting ready to dispense a pain pill I had what I can only describe as brain fog or thymentia, as we thyroid cancer patients call our lapses in cognitive function. I opened the locked narcotic drawer in my medication cart, took out the card of narcotics and the narc book, to record the withdraw. When I looked at the number of pills in the card and compared it to what was recorded in the narc book it was beyond my comprehension. The numbers in the book and the number of pills on the card weren't matching up to me. My stomach dropped. What is happening? I had just counted this drawer with the off going nurse hours before and everything was fine.

I looked at the book, scanned the card, back and forth several times. Simple math had escaped me. It took

27

several minutes of studying the numbers before I regained my senses.

I met with Dr. Jones a few weeks after my neck dissection. The appointment was to plan for my RAI, but I also brought up my recent incidence of brain fog. I was also feeling fatigued, which wasn't too surprising given I had just been through two major surgeries in less than 2 months. But, I just wasn't feeling like myself, in a lot of ways. Dr. Jones told me we could add a second thyroid replacement medication, T3, to supplement the T4 medication I was already taking. I was agreeable to try anything to help me feel normal again.

Dr. Jones explained RAI, also known as I-131 came in a capsule that I would swallow after preparing my body with two thyrogen injections to raise my TSH level. Thyroid cancer patient's TSH levels are kept very low, known as hyperthyroid, to suppress the growth or recurrence of the cancer. A normal TSH range would be from 0.4-4.0 ml u/L. Mine, as a cancer patient has been kept around 0.03 ml u/L. Raising the TSH level for RAI helps to stimulate any remaining thyroid tissue for the absorption of the RAI. Another option is to stop the thyroid replacement medication several weeks before the RAI. Each doctor has their own preference of which method to use.

In order for the RAI to be totally effective the body must be starved of iodine, thus starving the remaining thyroid cells so they are quick to take up all the radioactive iodine to kill any remaining cancer. This means LID, low iodine diet. It is one of the biggest challenges all thyroid cancer patients face. I was told to avoid any iodized salt, sea salt, seafood, dairy products, egg yolks, soy products, commercial bakery products, foods that contain red dye #3 and any vitamins or medications containing iodine. Meat was also limited to 6 oz. a day. The diet is limited and takes a creative imagination. I dropped 7 pounds in 2 weeks on the diet. I was working 6 days a week at my 2 jobs and relying on fast meals without a lot of thought put into them. Kelly mailed me a box of LID friendly foods; she was always sweet and thoughtful with whatever I needed to make my cancer journey easier. She was also researching and emailing information to me to help with my cancer struggles. Emails I never even saw until everything came crashing down and I was able to focus again.

There is plenty of information online in various sites and in support groups on social media. Although doctors will usually give a handout of the do's and don'ts of the diet I would encourage anyone that must do LID to take the time ahead of their diet to research their options. Otherwise, it can be quite frustrating having to always look at the ingredients of everything when you are starving.

March 2016

After finishing my 2 thyrogen injections and my low iodine diet I went to Dr. Jones' office and swallowed my radioactive iodine capsule. I also had to be 6 weeks out from my CT that I had prior to surgery in Seattle because of the iodine in the contrast. I was anxious to know when I could eat a normal diet again. Dr. Jones told me it would be alright to resume eating whatever I wanted by dinnertime that evening. Every doctor has their own guidelines regarding how long to stay on LID after RAI I've learned in online support groups. It ranges from 48 hours up to a week. Also, depending on the dosage of RAI, the endocrinologist will tell their patient guidelines for isolating away from other people and any preparations one can take for precautions of spreading any radiation into the home. I lived alone so I didn't have to worry about anyone else. My endocrinologist had me isolate for 5 days.

A lot of people complain of oral issues following RAI. This is an effect of the radiation drying us out. Our teeth and gums require moisture, i.e. saliva, to fight bacteria and decay. My dental office suggested I have my teeth cleaning prior to the RAI and that I brush fluoride onto my teeth during and several weeks after the RAI. My mom also suggested using a water flosser. I was quite shocked at how much flossing leaves behind that a water flosser will remove. These three things were essential in maintaining my oral health. I've read about many people getting cavities and cracked teeth after RAI, so precaution is a must.

During RAI it is suggested to suck on sours to extract the radiation from our salivary glands. A lot of the RAI will settle in the salivary glands. My dentist warned against the sugared lemon candy I wanted to use and suggested a sugar free alternative. But since being diagnosed with cancer I was now overly cautious of artificial sweeteners. I chose the sugared sours and just used my water flosser mixed with alcohol free mouthwash. To date I've not encountered any problems with my teeth. But I recently had a dream, or more of a nightmare, that I bit down on something and all my bottom teeth started to crack. And the more I continued to chew the more my teeth broke off and all fell out of my mouth. I woke up immediately in a panic feeling my teeth to see if they were all still intact. This shows how a trauma, like cancer, can impact our subconscious in the littlest of ways. People with a history of bad oral hygiene may not expect to have a successful outcome if they already have preexisting problems.

Five months after RAI I got a dreaded summer cold. I try to stay away from over the counter medications, but my constant drippy nose was a nuisance. So, I took an oral decongestant. Huge mistake! I didn't even consider the fact I'd just had radiation. The decongestant didn't help my nose much, but it did kick start my salivary glands to start acting up, or should I say, to barely act at all. Our salivary glands produce saliva essential for our oral health but also essential for when we eat. Saliva helps lubricate plus breaks down starches with the enzyme amylase. We have three sets of salivary glands which include parotid glands in front of the ears, and submandibular and sublingual glands located under the jaw. These glands drain saliva into our mouth through ducts. The Stenson ducts are connected to the parotids by the second molar and the Wharton ducts are connected to submandibular and sublingual on the floor of the mouth.

I watched an informative lecture online from a maxillofacial prosthodontist, or as he called himself, a cancer dentist, who confirmed radiation does scar the salivary glands and the ducts. Some people will be affected more than others depending on their treatment and genetics.

When I ate, my parotids, mainly the right, would swell with saliva. And because the ducts were scarred, the saliva couldn't drain and would continue to build pressure, causing immense pain. I would have to milk my gland, running my fingers down my cheek to try and empty the gland. This went on for several months off and on before it stopped being an issue. My parotids don't swell up anymore but also don't work at full capacity. Food usually sticks to my back teeth, especially breads and crackers. I am constantly using my finger to sweep food off my back teeth when I eat; very annoying and not too polite when out in public. I recently ate pretzels and didn't have the saliva to break them down. It was like chewing a wad of pretzel gum. *Still waiting to go on and live a normal life with this good cancer...*

Nine days after swallowing my I-131 pill I went to the nuclear medicine department at the hospital to have a whole-body scan. This would help to determine if any of the thyroid cancer had metastasized. Several days later I met with Dr. Jones to go over the results. The imaging report stated normal uptake within the nasal mucosa, salivary glands, liver, bowel, and in the neck. It also showed abnormal focus of intense activity below the liver and next to my bladder. Dr. Jones was confident it was all residual and nothing to worry about. But, when you have cancer, you do worry. I discussed my results with the physician I worked for and he asked a radiologist he had much respect for professionally, to look at my scan. The radiologist agreed on the cautious side and suggested I have further testing. Ugh. I was so overwhelmed at this point. No choice but to keep moving forward.

April 2016

Kelly flew up and we headed to Seattle to see Dr. Baugh for a second opinion regarding my recent scan. He wasn't overly anxious to assume the worst. He suggested we give the RAI a few more months to work then he would order a neck and abdominal CT as well as a PET scan. A PET scan is considered nuclear imaging as it uses a radioactive substance called a tracer that is administered intravenously. Dr. Baugh suggested I come back in three months for my scans. I agreed that was a reasonable time frame. Kelly mentioned wanting to come back with me for my upcoming scans. I felt guilty she was putting so much time and money out for all my medical issues. I told her she didn't have to come back for the testing. I didn't want her to think I expected her to be there for everything. But, I wasn't able to express my feelings in a loving and understandable way anymore. I couldn't feel empathetic to what Kelly was feeling and wanting. I was like a robot, going through the motions on autopilot. And the sad part is that I didn't realize just how numb I had become to everything. Because, if any of us were consciously aware we were acting so much differently from our normal personality we would be able to change it, right?

The next morning at the hotel I received a text from my previous relationship *ex* again. I had received texts checking in on my health every three to four weeks from this person as well as other people too. I knew it upset Kelly whenever my ex text me inquiring how I was doing, but I wanted Kelly to trust me, to trust us and what we meant to each other. I was dealing with so much stress with my cancer I didn't want to deal with the stress of telling anyone, even my ex, to leave me alone. The feeling in my heart was that wild horses couldn't drag me from Kelly, ever. But Kelly had a past with infidelities and wasn't able to trust. I felt like I was the one paying for all the indiscretions and bad behavior everyone else in her past had done to her. As time went on and this issue kept coming up, I became extremely frustrated. Trust is the foundation of any relationship and Kelly had no trust in me, in us. When the one you love doesn't trust you it can be soul crushing. She would always tell me "I love you more" when we said that to each other. She shared that she couldn't believe I was with her. But I also felt the same, I felt just as blessed to have her with me. I don't know if it was the fear of losing me to someone else or losing me to cancer, but Kelly wasn't able to be the emotional support I needed as she was just as afraid of what we were facing along with her own personal worries.

In a normal relationship setting when problems arise couples can communicate and try to find resolve. But when there is a major life event happening it will take priority, and not because of selfishness, but because people can only handle so much at a time. Plus, unbeknownst to me I was emotionally flatlining and Kelly was only responding to the changes she saw and felt in me. The attention and care she was used to getting had stopped. I would share with her on a few occasions that I didn't feel like myself anymore. She wanted me to seek counseling for depression. I dismissed her suggestions because I didn't feel depressed. I was eating, I was sleeping, and I was functioning day to day. But I was functioning on autopilot with anxiety and irritability only. I shared with a couple friends that I didn't feel like *me* anymore though I wasn't able to put my finger on how I felt displaced from myself. A nurse I've known and worked with for years recently told me that I'd changed after my first surgery; that I wasn't the same person. I asked her, "Why didn't you tell me?" She thought it was related to the stress from having cancer. She would handle me with kid gloves on several occasions when I would act out at work. My boss also on occasion was on the receiving end of my irritable responses. He also never called me out on my behavior. We always take our frustrations out on the people we are closest to and I was no exception. Kelly would later say to me, "Well you have a psychology degree, you couldn't see how you were acting?" Um, no...that may have been possible only if I could have extracted myself from my own body and watched myself from the sidelines. I had felt like I was all alone in this change until I saw a question from someone in a thyroid cancer support group ask, "Does anyone else feel like an alien has taken over your body?"

FIVE

Deeper into the Fog

June 2016

I was off to Nevada for a few days of relaxation with Kelly. She was always a selfless host, doing whatever I wanted to do when I visited. We had fun, but the dynamic of our relationship had changed. It didn't matter how many times I said "I love you" because I wasn't showing that love. Emotionally I was just going through the motions. I wasn't conscious of how distanced I'd become; the ache I felt deep in my soul just to be next to her, the pride I felt that she was with me and the way I would constantly hug her and drive her nuts was gone. Kelly never pushed me to look at my behavior or lack thereof, and who knows if she did if I would have even been receptive to listen. She suffered in silence which only led for resentment to build up.

I flew home and headed to Seattle for my scans. I had my PET scan first. I was started on an IV for the contrast to be injected. The most common being a radioactive substance of glucose (sugar), the tracer.

Because cancer cells use more glucose than normal cells the uptake of the tracer is more prominent on the scan if cancer is detected. Once the PET scan was over I had to drink two bottles of barium contrast to prepare for my abdominal CT. I got that down, barely, and started another IV for the CT contrast for the neck scan. I met with Dr. Baugh a couple hours later to get my results. NED, no evidence of disease. I felt relief, in a sense, but once you've had cancer you know it is likely there will be more scans and more tests, so I couldn't let myself think this would be the last time I'd go through this.

August 2016-January 2017

After getting a clean bill of health at my last appointment I settled back into my day to day routine. I had been working 6-7 days a week at my 2 jobs for several years, so I resumed back to my schedule. I continued to struggle with memory issues although at the time I didn't realize I was so off from myself. I was forgetting at times, little details at work. My boss would ask why I hadn't written his surgeries on his calendar and I assumed it was only a small oversight, again and again. While getting lunch for a friend at work, who I knew detested mayonnaise and told me "Do not order my sandwich with the mayo spread if they ask." What did I do? I ordered her sandwich with the mayo spread. When I was standing at the counter ordering my mind was a cluster of confusion of what she had told me not 30 minutes earlier. I was missing my chiropractic and hair appointments because I had the wrong dates and times written down. I was so frustrated and sure it was the other people screwing up but looking back it was all me. I'd never missed my appointments before, ever. Kelly was telling me that I was saying things in conversation that I had no recollection of. It was like I was on a mind-altering drug. But the only drug I was taking was the synthetic thyroid medication.

Several years earlier when I was in the emergency room for a hernia I was given dilaudid, a powerful narcotic. The doctor was going to attempt to push my hernia back through the abdominal wall, so he ordered a high dose of pain medication beforehand. While waiting for the dilaudid to kick in I was texting with a nurse I worked with to tell her that I was in the ER and that I may not be into work the next day. I felt as clear and focused as I normally did, carrying on a conversation with her. Well, she was laughing the next time I saw her. She told me I was making no sense during our conversation because I was so out of it on the pain medication. Yet, in my memory I was as clear as day. As clear as day as I assumed I was this whole time after I lost my thyroid…

Kelly continued to apply for positions in her field closer to me. She wasn't having much luck and was growing frustrated. I knew she didn't want to stay where she was, so I never offered to move to her, plus I was hesitant to move too far from my doctors at this stage in my health. Even though I was cleared of any disease on my last visit with Dr. Baugh I wanted to make absolute certain I was going to stay that way. After the misdiagnosis from Dr. Smith, I had full confidence in Dr. Baugh and was afraid to put my trust in anyone new if I moved.

We continued to travel back and forth. And my anxiety and irritability continued to grow with a problem neighbor that had a steady stream of riff raff visitors and the smell of drugs seeping into my condo on a regular basis. This would bother anyone to a point, but I let it consume me. This just helped keep me on edge all the time. Kelly was up for a visit and got upset about my ex again. I couldn't remember the last time I had even received a text, but Kelly felt that I hadn't being respectful of her feelings. And given a different situation, i.e. no cancer, I would have most likely done whatever it took to make her happy and feel secure, but I couldn't rationalize her feelings nor my own thoughts. I had anxiety through the roof. I yelled at Kelly to drop it. I couldn't communicate with compassion and empathy anymore because I couldn't feel those emotions. Whatever I tried to explain or communicate to her came out wrong. We never got any resolve because neither one of us was willing to budge on our positions. And once any conversation was over it never entered my mind again. I didn't think back and feel sad, bad, remorseful, happy, nothing. I wasn't processing feelings and information like I used to. There was no reflecting on my thoughts. I was on to the next thing,

45

whatever that may be. We kept going forward with our relationship but there were cracks forming in our foundation. I was oblivious to it all.

I hadn't been sleeping well the past few months. The RAI had dried out more than my salivary glands. I couldn't get any air through my nose so I was waking up at nightwith my mouth wide open but that was drying out too. It was miserable. And dangerous, a total open gateway for spiders to crawl in...

I decided on another surgery. My septum was slightly deviated which had never bothered me before and my turbinates (structures in the nose that warm and humidify air we breathe) were dry and swollen. I would lie down in bed and my nose would completely block off. I had my boss examine my nose and he agreed that a surgery would help with my breathing. He offered to do the procedure, given that I trusted him to do it. Of course, I did. I wouldn't have worked for a doctor I had no respect for. I scheduled my septoturbinoplasty and Kelly flew up to help me through the recovery. Surgery went well and to date I have a clear nose, and to my knowledge, haven't swallowed any spiders in the night.

The presidential election was in full swing. My whole existence to this point was an aversion to politics. But, the new agitated me was 101% drawn in. I was all over social media giving my two cents and absorbing any new information I could. Not even this total turnaround in my usual disdain for politics made me clue in that I was not the same old me. (Now that I am back to *me*, I have resumed my previous aversion to politics)

Kelly came back the following month to spend the Christmas holiday with my family. She had offered to make some of their gifts and to get the rest at craft fairs. All I had to do was write a check for part of it. She always kept one step ahead of me making sure everything was taken care of.

Kelly's parents were also in town for the holiday, so we were able to spend time with them as well. Her grandfather had fallen and was recuperating in a rehab facility. He seemed to be doing well despite not wanting to be away from his own home. Kelly had always been close to her grandfather, traveling home routinely over the years to make sure he was taken care of. He was quite a character.

Christmas day came. I should have been on top of the world. I had the love of my life beside me. I'd dreamt of this for years. But I was only going through the motions now. I wasn't able to feel excited anymore. Kelly bought me everything under the sun for Christmas. She spared no expense or thought when it came for doing for me. I was that spoiled kid with fifty presents under the tree.

At my parents we were all opening gifts. Everyone was thrilled as Kelly did a great job on her handmade gifts. Sometimes I wondered if my family loved Kelly more than me; they thought the world of her. As my family was opening their gifts they were all assuming everything was just from Kelly. I felt immediately insulted that I wasn't recognized. And because I had no filter anymore I made it clear that I too was involved in the gifts. My family looked at me as if I had two heads. No one knew what to say. I became paranoid that Kelly was trying to overshadow me with my own family. I was clueless how ridiculous I was acting. My paranoia continued to the next holiday when I was hesitant to do combined gifts again with Kelly with friends.

Kelly flew back home after the holiday and shortly thereafter her grandfather passed away. It was a shock as everyone thought he was doing well with his rehab. I don't remember being there for her in the way I should have been. She needed me, and I was emotionally absent.

SIX

Downward Spiral

April 2017

It was time for my follow up with Dr. Jones. She wanted an ultrasound to check for suspicious lymph nodes. The imaging report showed abnormalities with my left submandibular salivary gland with possible lymph node involvement. *Here we go again with this good cancer…*

I called Dr. Baugh's office. He wanted me to have a neck CT with contrast and follow up with him in Seattle. The CT imaging report read that there were no changes from the last scan, so nothing was of concern. I headed to Seattle anyway. Sitting in Dr. Baugh's office he brought my CT up on his screen. Despite what the imaging report stated, Dr. Baugh did see something of concern. He pointed to an area behind my right carotid artery and said, "See right there? There is something there, but I can't tell exactly what it is. I think it's small enough we can watch it for now." Dr. Baugh was hesitant to do exploratory surgery so close to my carotid

51

artery, and I agreed we should watch it for now. He suggested follow up in a year unless something changed.

Dr. Jones was checking my thyroglobulin levels (thyroid protein tumor marker) every six months and it hadn't been going up. It wasn't at zero, but it was less than two. This was my new norm as a cancer patient. TSH lab checks every three months or more depending on if my levels are stable. Constant adjusting of medications to balance out TSH level. Thyroglobulin checks every six months to see if *the good cancer* is coming back. Doctor appointments every six months, ultrasounds once or twice a year, and so on…

Summer 2017

My anxiety was continuing to climb along with my thymentia. One evening while on the phone with Kelly I was multi-tasking as I always did or tried to do. Kelly had given me a fancy knife at Christmas for slicing vegetables for my juicer. I was attempting to put the knife back into the protective sleeve it was kept in after washing it, only I couldn't figure out which way it went in. The knife is curved, and one side of the sleeve was open, so it really didn't require rocket science to know how to put it on. I kept trying to force it in backwards despite it not wanting to go. I became increasingly frustrated and forced it in anyway. Kelly tried to talk me down from my anxiety, but I couldn't be rationalized with, not from her, not from anyone. I felt like I was seriously losing it at times.

At work, my boss shared with me that the competing medical practice in town that Dr. Smith worked for had offered to buy his clinic and he was selling to them. Our clinic had been one of the last independent practices left, and in this day and age of evolving healthcare, it was increasingly difficult for small physician owned medical practices to compete with large corporate medical practices. My plan was to leave after the buyout at the end of the year and go full time at my second job. I knew Kelly would eventually find a position close to home and I would move with her once she was settled. Still, it was hard knowing my time with my clinic family was nearing the end.

September 2017

Kelly was becoming increasingly frustrated. I had an old friend staying with me after a family medical emergency and I wasn't as present for Kelly as I normally was, or assumed I was. She was questioning why I was acting differently towards her since my friend arrived. I wasn't able to soothe her insecurities as I only became defensive whenever questioned about anything. In my mind I knew that I was completely overwhelmed with trying to be supportive for my friend and it made me upset Kelly was questioning me. I was rigid in my position when she tried to talk things over. Per my new norm I had no empathy to her position. I too was frustrated and didn't know how to make things right, how to make Kelly feel secure about our relationship. We agreed to be more open with our concerns in the future, but we hadn't really resolved anything. The physical, as well as emotional distance between us, was too overwhelming for Kelly, and understandably so.

October 2017

Kelly and I went on a trip to Maui that she had planned earlier in the year. Early in our relationship we dreamt about being married on the beach there someday. With everything that had happened with my health we hadn't discussed marriage in quite some time. We arrived in Maui and were excited to be there, but I continued to be my usual anxiety ridden and irritated self. It wasn't the romantic vacation we had originally envisioned it to be. I couldn't enjoy time with Kelly. I couldn't enjoy life. I couldn't even enjoy Maui.

November 2017

Kelly drove up for Thanksgiving. Her mom was experiencing serious medical issues and she needed to look into some extra care for her. I had started working extra shifts at my second job in preparation for my transition to go full time. I was exhausted and pushing limits with my health. Kelly didn't want me doing it and was rightfully concerned, but I felt I needed to help both of my employers. I put their needs ahead of my own health. Kelly had her hands full with her mom and I was running on empty, emotionally and physically.

We had a serious conversation after I hurt Kelly's feelings, on a few different things during this visit. My harsh approaches to her had increased along with my irritability. I was devoid of any loving emotion. She became defensive and cried and I became defensive and stayed mad and insulted. I wasn't even able to console her as she sobbed and told me "I love you with all my heart." I was completely numb. The love of my life sat sobbing right next to me and I felt nothing. Again, she left for home with no real resolve to our widening gap in our relationship.

January 15, 2018

"My feelings have changed." That's all I can remember Kelly saying on the other end of the phone that day. I didn't feel sadness or surprise. I may have been in shock, but my only reply was "It is what it is." It was over. Two and a half years of a love story that struggled to survive, did not.

The next night I realized what had just happened. Kelly and I were done. I grew increasingly anxious and messaged her repeatedly to rethink her decision. No response. Six days later I received a response after threatening to fly down to see her in person. Kelly was done and wanted time alone to rediscover herself and told me I was "broken" and that I had broken her heart too many times. I pleaded with her, but she was done. Is she right? Am I broken? I knew I was irritable a lot, but broken? I contacted a psychologist I'd seen several years earlier after my previous unhealthy relationship ended. I needed an opinion of someone who knew me, a professional opinion. I spent the next several weeks trying to go on each day. There were days I got less than two hours sleep and would have to go into work. I was so nauseated I could barely eat. I dropped 17 pounds.

February 2018

I started reflecting on the beginning of our relationship and how over the top in love I was with Kelly. When had that changed and why? Why had I become so irritable at times? Where did my desire for her go? What happened to my passion for a fulfilling life? I looked at the timeline of when I started to change. It all happened after my first surgery. I started researching my thyroid medication. I had to dig deep as the side effects I was experiencing were considered less common. There they were in black and white: Irritability, false or unusual sense of well-being, feelings of suspicion or distrust, mental depression, quick to overreact emotionally, anxiety and emotional lability. I also researched the symptoms of being hyperthyroid, as we cancer patients are kept, to suppress any cancer from returning. Thyroid levels can have extreme effects on mood as well. I decided that I would look into the medication side effects first. I researched alternatives which led me to a natural thyroid replacement desiccated medication made from pig thyroid. Many of the people that switched to the desiccated medication swore by it. The main complaints from people after thyroid removal were either emotional and mental or physical such as weight gain and hair loss. I would have picked packing on a few extra pounds any day over the hell I'd experienced. It was noted in what I'd read that most doctors do not like desiccated medications as they are harder to regulate regarding our TSH than the synthetics. Since the synthetics are man-made there are specific amounts of ingredients the doctors can rely on. They also contain fillers that can cause adverse reactions. The desiccated medication I wanted to try included natural T4 and T3.

I messaged Dr. Jones right away and explained what had been happening with me and my emotions. I had asked her the previous year regarding my decreased libido and any relation it may have to my medication. She dismissed that theory and I never questioned it again, just thinking it was all related to my missing thyroid and I would be a different person for the rest of my life. So, I wasn't sure how she would react to my request for a change now. She got back to me right away and was honest about her feelings about desiccated medications but was willing to prescribe it to see if my symptoms went away.

Within the first couple days of starting the desiccated medication I noticed a change. My mind was becoming clearer. I could sit down in the quiet of the night and hear my own thoughts. I didn't feel as on edge. I was beginning to feel like *me* again, but the anxiety and irritability I had carried for so long were now being replaced with sadness and heartbreak. My emotions were now coming back, and I was feeling the loss from Kelly more than ever. I had woken from a bad dream into a horrible nightmare.

I finally got to meet with my psychologist, Sarah. I was anxious to hear her thoughts on my story. "Well Janelle, you've been through a lot. You shouldn't be so hard on yourself." Sarah explained how the cancer diagnosis itself is enough to send someone into an emotional tailspin, which I knew, but when you yourself are the one spinning, rationality is spinning downward with you. I told Sarah about my emotional side effects and how I was already feeling more myself after changing to the desiccated medication. I had also mentioned how I wasn't able to communicate effectively with Kelly and how my mind and judgement had been so clouded.

Sarah brought to my attention something I had never considered. General anesthesia. I know, as a nurse, that general anesthesia can affect the elderly but never have been told about the effects on younger people. As patients know, we are put to sleep for surgery and are under the watch of an anesthesiologist who will monitor vital signs and what cocktail of drugs to give to make us unaware of the pain and trauma our body undergoes during a surgical procedure.

Technically, general anesthesia doesn't put one to sleep. It induces a pharmacological coma. Anesthetics activate memory loss receptors in the brain. Communication between nerve cells for cognitive function and memory are disrupted. Sarah explained how it can take up to a year before all the nerves in the brain reconnect. And I had three major surgeries within a year's time. It was all starting to make sense to me. A nurse practitioner that my friend works for suggested that had I consulted with her prior to surgery she would have had me start on specific supplements to help with the effects of the anesthesia.

So many things I wish I had known prior to surgeries and medications and treatments. So much information that is not given to us thyroid cancer patients. I felt cheated. Cheated by God, by the doctors, by my own fate.

I was eager to tell Kelly what I had discovered. I wanted her to realize that I wasn't "broken" after all. I wrote her a letter explaining everything. I also messaged her but received no response to either attempt. I waited another couple of weeks and messaged her again. I received a response this time. Kelly was understanding and listened to my discovery about why I'd changed but was standoffish and resentful that it had taken so long for me to figure myself out. I booked a last-minute flight to surprise Kelly and plead my case. I just knew if she realized how sorry I was, sorry I'd changed, sorry I'd gotten cancer and been so messed up on medication, sorry I couldn't realize it until now, she would be open to us again. But Kelly was already closed off to me and to us. A few weeks later when I made one last attempt, Kelly told me she was seeing someone else. I could hear the resentment in her voice. She told me our time together was "More bad than good," and she had wanted to end it long before she did. She told me that her new person "actually wanted to do things with her" and that "I hadn't kept the promises I'd made to her in the beginning of our relationship." We were done for good. What started out so full of love and hope ended up with broken resentment and someone else in my place in her heart.

April-May 2018

I continued to see Sarah to help heal emotionally. I was getting better each day despite my broken heart. I was now feeling a sense of calm I hadn't known in way too long. It is hard to explain what it is like to have your mind so disconnected from yourself that you are not able to enjoy your own existence.

I met with Dr. Jones the first time since changing my medication. I let her know how much better I felt and how appreciative I was that she was willing to try the change for me despite her professional preference. I was curious, her thoughts on how many people experience the mental and emotional side effects as I did on the synthetic medication. She wasn't quick to admit to the downfalls of the synthetic medication as she was more to the side effects being related to the suppression of TSH. Although she did admit that every patient has a different reaction and different preference to which medication works best for their emotional and physical well-being as well as brain function. She told me if we were able to regulate my TSH on the desiccated medication she would keep me on it. I let her know we would need to get it as close as we could as I would not be going off this new medication, ever. I would never go back to the synthetic. My life depended on it. To this date we are still attempting to adjust my levels. I'm even more hyperthyroid on the desiccated medication which explains it was only the synthetic medication causing my emotional symptoms, not my TSH level, and I've never felt better and more me.

SEVEN

There is Nothing Good About Cancer. Nothing.

It takes a selfless, mentally strong and emotionally secure person to care for and be with a loved one dealing with cancer. Partners of cancer patients may have the best intentions but are rarely aware of the emotional toll it will take on them as well. As soon as we are diagnosed it becomes all about us, but our partners are dealing with many fears and insecurities too. The whole dynamic of the relationship changes. We don't intend to not meet the needs of our partners but how can we when we cannot even meet our own? We automatically expect them to support us through our worst, after all, they are there with us through our best.

In the beginning having support through doctor's visits, surgeries and treatments, while daunting at times, is doable, there is always more to contend with emotionally. Not one of my doctors ever mentioned the importance of seeking counseling or support for me or my partner. Is this because I only had the good cancer?

Cancer patients, don't mean to be selfish, ill-tempered, distant, moody, worrisome, anxious, fatigued, disagreeable or less motivated. However, we are greatly affected by our cancer diagnosis, body disfiguring surgeries and medications and treatments that alter us physically, emotionally and mentally. All this along with the fact we've been forced to face our own mortality sooner than we'd ever expected too.

The first time my neck was cut into to remove my thyroid it left a one and a half-inch scar. It wasn't too noticeable. It didn't bother me. The second surgery less than two months later to strip out the cancerous lymph nodes left me with a four and a half-inch scar. It looked like something right out of a slasher movie. To me, the operated side of my neck appeared caved in. Dr. Baugh told me that he had made the incision along the crease of my neck to make it less noticeable. But it was very noticeable to me. All I saw was a four and a half-inch defect on an already aging forty-six-year-old neck. I now hated the way I looked in v neck tops because all I focused on was my scar. At one point during our relationship Kelly suggested that we skype so we could see each other instead of just talking on the phone every day. I shot that idea down right away, although I never told her why. I knew what I saw when I looked at myself and I knew that skype images can make someone look even more distorted. Kelly was always telling me how beautiful and perfect my body was, so why would I give her extra opportunity to see how disfigured I'd become? I felt that Kelly had me up on a pedestal, not that I thought I needed to be on one, but I certainly didn't want to be knocked off of it, because there is no way back up once you fall.

When Kelly ended our relationship, she told me "I could have dealt with everything if it was just the cancer." But everything happened the way it happened because of the cancer. Cancer's effects on a relationship are insidious. Recently I've connected with many wonderful people through a few thyroid cancer support sites I'm a part of. What I've found are so many others that are struggling with their emotional health and relationships the same as I had. Both men and women, and of all nationalities, are affected the same. People that state their personality has changed, that they are now short tempered with their family members, that they have lost their filter, their sex drive is gone, they have crippling anxiety, memory issues, lack of motivation and so on. One woman shared with me her husband was ready to leave her because he was tired of having to deal with her anxiety. The problem with sharing these symptoms with doctors is that they will often just prescribe other medications, anti-anxiety and antidepressants to mask the emotional problems. One woman was told by her doctor, "I'm not here to make you feel good, I'm here to keep you alive." But, what they (doctors) fail to realize is that we want quality of life too, not just breathing and existing. The quality of life we had prior to having our thyroids taken. The quality of life we were told would not change with our thyroid gone. The quality of life we were told would stay the same with a pill instead of a functioning gland that we were born with; that existed in us for a reason. Thus far, across the board, I've learned we thyroid cancer patients are all given the same line from our doctors, "You have the good cancer. With your thyroid gone you will take a pill and go on to live a normal life. You won't miss it (thyroid gland)." Are they all learning from the same expired textbook? Because what we are told is so far from the truth.

We, as individuals, are all different; different in our genetic make-up and the way our bodies respond to medications, foods, environment, etc. So, to replace a gland with a thyroid replacement pill is not a one size fits all solution. There are synthetic hormone replacement medications, which seems to be choice #1 for doctors after thyroidectomy, and there are natural hormone replacement medications, desiccated, which many doctors are against. Since discovering my emotional downfall was related to my generic synthetic medication I was curious to what others were experiencing. Many like myself found *themselves* again after switching to the desiccated medication. Many had physical symptoms like weight gain and hair loss after switching and opted for the name brand synthetic vs the generic. And some claim to do well on the generic synthetic. Again, it is not

69

a one size fits all. We cancer survivors must be our own advocates for our health.

Many relationships fail at the hands of all types of cancer. The patient and their partner have so much to face with the initial shock of the diagnosis, that they don't take into consideration the emotional aspects cancer will have on their relationship. People assume their love will survive anything. But it won't, it can't, because we are only human, and people can only take so much in before they break. Soon after my second surgery Kelly brought up my health insurance. She was so detail and task oriented, she wanted to make sure I was covered in the best way possible considering my new way of life with doctor appointments and tests. I think this along with other things she tried to help with, was her way of trying to have control over a situation that she had no control over. Neither of us did. But, I didn't care about what better plan was available or want to think about money at all at that moment. All I heard was "You need to go to HR and ask about a health savings account..." before I shut her down. All I felt at that moment was her coming at me with, do this, do that, not this way, do it that way. I was not able to handle a simple discussion. I couldn't process anything in my mind. I think this is the first time I hurt her feelings and saw her cry. So, as time went on and I was not able to process feelings and communicate effectively, Kelly became resentful and gave up. Can I really blame her? Not really. Does it hurt that she thought it easier to move on to someone new without any cancer baggage? Absof*ckinglutely. But she chose what was best for her at the time with my pedestal image now shattered.

I stress to anyone diagnosed with cancer to make counseling a priority at the beginning of your diagnosis. Any psychologist worth their salt could be instrumental in helping keep you and your partner emotionally on track during your cancer journey. The many emotions of fear, anxiety, resentment, uncertainty, depression and stress that accompany cancer are better dealt with a professional. Regular relationship stressors will inevitably take a backseat even after treatment has ended and couples are trying to resume back to the dynamic of what they had, because the one affected from cancer will

71

still be processing what they have just been through. Intimacy usually takes a backseat as well and this causes friction and resentment with the partner who may question the lack of motivation from the cancer patient. This is a common complaint with many after having their thyroids removed. My situation was no different unfortunately. I was obviously aware my sex drive was gone but trying to rationally process that one issue with everything else in my head was impossible at the time. Thyroid cancer patients have no clue, on how many levels, the impact losing their thyroid will have on them and their personal lives after the dust has settled from treatment. This is because we are told by our doctor that we won't miss our thyroid being removed. I wish I had the insight at the time of my first surgery to have researched all the possible pitfalls of a thyroidectomy. Although just dealing with the initial cancer diagnosis is quite overwhelming in itself.

EIGHT

FOR THE PARTNER

Please Don't Resent Us for Having Cancer

The saying "You don't know what anyone else is going through unless you've walked in their shoes" is true

I've read that some 50% of relationships dissolve during a cancer diagnosis. And that women are six times more likely to be left than men. The younger the person (partner) and less time they have invested in the relationship are the ones more likely to leave sooner than the older person with more years with their cancer partner. There are also the cases where the relationship was in failure before the diagnosis despite the age and time factor.

You may be at the start of your partner's diagnosis, scared and with questions but determined to stand by their side or you may be further along, dealing with the struggles of your partner's treatments and emotions. Whatever stage you are in, I urge you to find a

73

counselor/psychologist trained in helping with couples and illness. If professional services are not affordable for you, then look in to joining a support group with people that are experiencing the same. Don't rely on well-meaning advice from a friend or family member that has taken a couple psychology courses at their local college as their opinions can be biased towards you as well as their own preconceived notions. You require someone that has the education and understanding of how a serious illness affects a couple, so that you may get the right support needed to maneuver through the difficult road ahead, and it will be difficult. You will need ongoing support and guidance. This will test your love for your partner like nothing you can imagine. Cancer is not sexy. Cancer is not a walk in the park. Cancer is selfish. Cancer will expose your partner's weaknesses and vulnerabilities as well as your own. The mystery of what attracted you to your partner in the beginning will be replaced with the raw truth of who they can become in their worst times.

If you are married and took vows with your partner, remember what you promised with those vows. To be with you for better or worse, to love you in sickness and in health, for richer or poorer, to love and cherish. Real love is unconditional. No one chooses cancer. You may reach a point thinking that your own feelings are not validated and become resentful. A lot of people choose to go outside of their relationship to get their emotional and physical needs met because their partners are too sick and distracted to meet them. I'm astonished at how many people leave their sick partner to replace them with a healthier person. Not everyone stays healthy forever, whether through disease, injury or with Father Time. So, you too, or your next partner, could become ill and dependent to be loved and cared for through a difficult time. You can look at it one of two ways. You can stay and fight for the person you originally chose to love and remember why you chose them to begin with, or you can take a gamble on a new partner, that may or may not remain perfect and healthy to your expectations.

If you do choose to stay, along with counseling, you should have strong social support as well. Good friends are essential. Don't spend all your free time sitting at home and worrying about your situation. Kelly told me in one of our last conversations that she sat home alone every weekend for two years and worried about me. She stated, "But that's on me I guess." She was resentful. Unfortunately, she did not have a strong social support of friends where she was at. She had no outlet for her emotions and worries with anyone that knew of the complexities this illness brings to a relationship. So, it is most important to get out with your friends or family and distract yourself regularly whether through physical exercise or emotional support.

Cancer will test the emotional strength of the person affected and everyone closely involved, guaranteed. Given you know what you are up against and can prepare for the journey and remember what brought you together in the first place, it can be a life changing event to appreciate each other, and life, all the more.

NINE

Cancer's Dirty Little Secret

Abandonment. While it is somewhat understandable knowing the reasons behind partner abandonment during cancer, it is not as understandable to know why family and friends remove themselves from the cancer patient's life as well. Yes, that is right. The very people that we expect to always be by our side, despite whatever befalls us, cannot, or do not want to deal with another's illness. It is well known as cancer's dirty little secret in the cancer community.

One of my closest friends told me, "Friendship is like a marriage, you should be there always, for better or worse, in sickness and in health." This is a friend that I have known for thirty years. A friend I have endured good times with as well as bad. All relationships, at some point, will experience struggles of some sort, whether intimate, friends or family. Because we are all human, we are selfish at certain times then selfless at other times, with most of us trying to learn from our experiences and mistakes along the way.

My friend that made this statement has dealt with a congenital heart issue all her life and recently underwent open heart surgery at 48 years old. She understands what it is like to have a serious medical issue disrupt your life, she knows the feeling of facing your own mortality at an early age. But many people, *healthy* people, that have never experienced more than a bad sinus infection or a broken bone, don't understand *sick* people. They don't know what it is like to deal with not feeling good physically or emotionally, to always be in your head with worries about how your illness will affect the rest of your life, with quality of life and relationships and financial security. It is easier to gain understanding from people that truly know what it is like to struggle with a health issue. I've witnessed someone with cancer have unbelievable strong support from family and friends and I've also witnessed another treated rather terribly by family and friends.

It seems as if some people view illness as a weakness, a character flaw, that someone isn't willing to overcome and fit in with societies agenda of being active and happy. Being sick is not attractive. People prefer to be around others who do not remind them of unpleasantries. And a lot of people's moods are dependent on those around them, so they gravitate towards the good time friends or family. They see sick people as complainers and malingerers. Usually people will offer their condolences at the beginning of someone's diagnosis then move on with their lives as if it is a one-time event like a cold or broken arm that will be treated and resolved. Some of the neediest people are the first to flee, not wanting the sick person to take attention from them. And some just have their own biased beliefs that keep them from having compassion to another's struggles. Many thyroid cancer survivors have stated that friends and family are mad at them for being sick, telling them to "Get over it already, it's not like you're dying." Shockingly, many people with all types of cancer report being suddenly blocked from all forms of communication with particular friends and family, with no clue why, only their cancer diagnosis. Some cancer survivors have had people completely disappear from their lives during treatment then suddenly reappear after they were deemed well again.

Cancer will eventually wear out its welcome with many. Friends and family expect the cancer patient to return to their former self after treatment. Some don't care to hear about the particulars of your journey. They expect the old you back. That is impossible. We will never be the same. Illness changes people. Self-reflection is huge, once one has recovered from the trauma of treatment and regains their emotional and mental capacity. Reflection of everyone else is also huge. Life becomes too short for fair weather friends and family. Life and health and spirituality take on whole new meanings. Cancer patients don't want to be burdensome or pitied or shunned, just to be understood and respected. Fighting cancer is a battle that only a true cancer warrior can understand.

TEN

FOR THE DOCTORS

Why Exactly is Thyroid Cancer the Best Cancer?

"How can we minimize another's experience having never experienced it ourselves?"

No one can ever prepare for a cancer diagnosis. It is one of the most single devastating things a person can be told. Why do you (doctors) continue to tell patients, "You have the good cancer. Your life will not change with your thyroid gone." How can you actually say this time and time again to patients? Is this complete ignorance on your part because that is what you are being taught in medical school by outdated texts and outdated professors? Or are you just trying to minimalize our disease to make your professional life easier? Can you honestly tell yourself that after the first, fifth, twenty-second, or hundredth patient that has complaints of not feeling the same after a thyroidectomy from cancer, that their symptoms are not related to what has just been removed from their bodies? Something that has such significance it functions to control

81

everything from bowel movements to metabolism to mood to sex drive to heart function?

I can't begin to tell you how many comments I have read from thyroid cancer patients that have been told by others, "Oh, you have the good cancer. I have real cancer (i.e. breast, leukemia, etc.)" Where do people get the idea that thyroid cancer is not as serious as other cancers? The doctors. That is where. STOP. JUST. STOP. Take a few moments and really think about how a cancer diagnosis affects someone physically and emotionally and mentally. Doctors seem to be basing this theory of *good cancer* off of survival rates compared to other cancers. But, as you know, we thyroid cancer patients can still have recurrence and will always worry about recurrence just like any other cancer patient. We still have complications from medications and treatments. And people do die from thyroid cancer. I was recently contacted from a man from the other side of the world. We belong to the same online support group for alternative treatments. His aggressive hurthle cell thyroid cancer is not responding to conventional treatment. He has metastasis to his neck and lungs. He is only thirty-five years old, married, and desperate to find what everyone else is doing alternatively so he can try and save his own life. Cancer takes a huge toll on everyone diagnosed, regardless of where it originates from. When doctors discount our diagnosis, it leaves us unprepared for what we are facing. It sets us up for failure, thinking everything will be fine. *I have nothing to worry about because my doctor told me so.*

Years ago, while in nursing school I was in clinicals one day. I was working with patients undergoing colonoscopies. A patient's monitor started beeping. As I flew around the corner to see what the commotion was my immediate reaction was to focus on the monitor. The source of the beeping. My instructor asked me why I was looking at the monitor and not the patient. Of course, the numbers, vital signs, on the monitor are important but the patient's current state of well-being should be the first concern. How do they look, how are they feeling? Common sense really. So why, when so many thyroid cancer patients complain of not feeling well physically or emotionally, are doctor's intent on only focusing on numbers, i.e. TSH levels, and not the actual patient. All too often doctors tell their patients

83

that their current complaint of not feeling well is not thyroid related because their numbers are where they are supposed to be. Even when a full thyroid panel is run doctors will disregard symptoms onto anything else other than thyroid.

Cancer is cancer. Thyroid cancer patients deserve the same respect and seriousness as every other cancer patient. Always. The struggle is real, as noted in the comments of so many still suffering…

"I would encourage everyone to never use such an ignorant statement again, as there is no such thing as good cancer. My life has dramatically changed, physically, mentally and emotionally."

"I've been cardioverted multiple times since TT (total thyroidectomy)."

"Not having a thyroid has ruined me."

"Did anyone notice a change in their personality after a thyroidectomy?"

"I feel like having my thyroid out is going to ultimately ruin my marriage. I am not the same person as I believe it completely changed my personality. I changed into a nothing person."

"I have so much brain fog."

"My bloodwork is fine, yet I can't lose weight and I'm so tired, extremely irritable and emotional."

"I can't remember anything anymore."

"My doctor could not save my laryngeal nerve."

"My friend had secondary cancer post TT and died today."

"NP (natural) thyroid has saved my sanity."

"My hair keeps coming out in loads."

"Every day I am not the same person. Every day I am never going to be the same physically and mentally."

"What threw me over the edge was yelling at my kid for reading a book out loud."

"I am angry, irritated and belligerent."

"My husband totally changed. More anger and less tolerant of anything."

"I am a bitch now. I am annoyed by everyone. Days I hate people. None of these feelings can be controlled"

"I don't even recognize who I am anymore."

"I've just ruined a one-year relationship through being totally out of character."

"My doctor didn't tell me about any of this other shit I am going through. I hate how I feel."

"I accused my surgeon of removing my patience and filter along with my thyroid."

"I miss the old me every day. I trusted my doc when she said, 'It's the good cancer.' It robs us of our lives."

"I have not been the same since. It was like a bitch switch was turned on. Don't have any clue as to how to turn it off."

"My biggest fear is never feeling normal again."

"I was a hot mess and forty-seven different kinds of crazy on the synthetic."

"My teeth are chipping and cracking all the way to the root."

"Cancer had wrapped around my left vocal cord."

"My normal heart rate is between 60-70. Lately it has gone up, once to 144."

"Labs are normal but I'm still waking up with massive panic attacks."

"My friend died three months from diagnosis, I don't see what's so good about this cancer."

"Please tell me life gets better and I get my energy back."

"I have sleep apnea now."

"Usually I'm a pretty peaceful person but everyone and everything has been getting on my nerves lately."

"Anyone know of any doctor that will listen to symptoms rather than labs?"

"I was on synthetic and it made me feel like a lunatic."

"I just feel *off* too often. Every day is a surprise."

"I'm a whole new person and not in a good way."

"There are times I wish I could have kept my thyroid with the cancer."

"My biggest fear is not feeling like ME again."

"My biggest fear is recurrence."

"My surgeon botched my TT resulting in bilateral laryngeal nerve damage."

"I am a shell of who I once was. This good cancer is the gift that keeps on giving."

"I don't have patience anymore. I have no tolerance. I hate it."

"I have uncontrollable anger."

"Nobody discusses the fact that quality of life post thyroid cancer is extremely poor for many."

"Sometimes I feel I'm going mad."

"It can be discouraging to know you are broken."

"My moods swing like Jekyll and Hyde."

"Since losing my thyroid I have to fight with myself to have patience. I have to fight myself not to snap and snarl at people."

"I have always thought it was unfortunate the doctors didn't understand the side effects of losing your thyroid. I've experienced extreme fatigue, weight gain, and personality changes."

"My other half says I don't listen to him and forgets I have these issues (thyroid) and claims I am careless about our relationship."

"The feelings of paranoia are very common. The fact is the thyroid has tremendous effects on the mind."

"There is nothing good about it other than it typically does have a higher survival rate, but that doesn't mean we don't feel what we feel."

ELEVEN

Here We Go Again II

September 2018

Dr. Jones' nurse called me with the results of my latest ultrasound, "You have a right upper cervical lymph node, a right mid cervical lymph node behind the carotid artery that would be difficult to access, two lymph nodes in the left lower cervical region, one of which is behind the carotid. These findings are suspicious. Do you want to schedule an FNA?" Hmm... Do I want a needle inserted that close to my carotid artery? Uh no, so I just asked her straight up, "Tell me, do they contain microcalcifications?" (a sign of cancer as my last cancerous nodes removed did contain microcalcifications). "Yes, I'm so sorry to have to give you this news Janelle. Are you headed back to Seattle to see Dr. Baugh? We'll forward your imaging to him."

Since my RAI in 2016, my thyroglobulin (protein tumor marker) had slowly but steadily gone down, reaching 1.1 this last March. Dr. Jones had always believed I still had cancer hiding somewhere because my number never went down to zero, but Dr. Baugh told me there was a chance it could just be residual thyroid tissue causing the result. Since I had trust in both of them this left me in a conundrum. But my scans weren't showing anything of immediate concern, so my only real option was to wait and see. Now I am left wondering, is this another bout of bad fate or did I do this to myself?

After my relationship ended I barely slept, and I barely ate, and once I found out Kelly had started a new relationship I began investing in premium vodka, a lot of it. Not good habits for a recovering cancer patient. I remember back to when Christie's relationship ended. She went through a phase of smoking cigarettes and drinking a lot of coconut rum. I recall saying to her, "What the hell are you doing? You have cancer!" She went through her well-deserved grieving phase and got back on track with her organic diet, alkaline water and supplement regimen. But the years following until her death she suffered with more personal stressors which, more than likely, added to the detriment of her health.

I had already decided after my last treatment of RAI that I was never subjecting my body to that again. Not that I had any side effects during the actual treatment, although the low iodine diet to prepare for it, made me a starved mad woman. It was the after effects of my damaged salivary glands that made my decision to look at alternative options given ever faced with cancer again, and surprise, here I am. I have seen one too many comments from people with cracked and necrotic teeth years out from treatment. There is also a risk of secondary cancers from RAI. When we swallow a radioactive capsule, it travels through our system and that itself is concerning to do just one time, let alone two or three. Given my first treatment was considered a high dose due to the extent of the cancer in my nodes, I am not willing to risk a second treatment despite any dose. And obviously, it didn't do such a bang-up job the first time otherwise I wouldn't have this recurrence now. This is strictly a personal decision and I would never discourage another cancer patient to do whatever treatment they feel is right for them. However, I do encourage empowering yourself with the knowledge of your situation and all options you have available to give your body what it requires to fight, as there is no one specific cure all for this disease.

A couple days before I was to consult with Dr. Baugh a friend sent me a link to a docuseries about cancer. She told me it was fate that it came up on her social media that day. She was right. I watched the first three out of the nine episodes before I met with Dr. Baugh. There were interviews with physicians and testimonials from cancer survivors regarding conventional treatment versus natural. This helped solidify my decision. I had already researched some natural cancer fighting protocols during my previous bout and had incorporated a couple of them, but once I thought I was *out of the cancer woods,* I became lazy with my juicing and the other things I was doing. I had reached a point that I felt like I was choking on all the pills I was taking so I only took my synthetic thyroid, the one least beneficial to my emotional state and decision making at the time. All it did was keep me alive and barely functioning.

Truthfully, the first time I was diagnosed I wasn't prepared emotionally. The second time, I wasn't prepared emotionally or mentally. By the time I had my second surgery I was not the same person. I recall my extreme irritability at nothing and at everything. As time went on my mind felt so full at times that I couldn't process information. The best way to describe it, is like my brain was short circuiting. My *wires* were connecting at some points but sparking at others. I had researched other treatments for my cancer through online articles and groups and invested in a couple of great books, none of which I followed through with completing educating myself with. One moment I had the drive for something, and the next moment it was all gone in a flash with no looking back. I couldn't sustain my thoughts. I remember Kelly telling me a time or two of an informative email she had sent to help with my many cancer difficulties. I never saw any of those until she left me, and my mind was clear enough to sort through my inbox. Now that I am psychologically back to myself, pre-cancer, I have my mind back, and the mind is the most powerful thing we have.

I met with Dr. Baugh. It was nice to see him considering the circumstances. He was the same professional guy with the soft demeanor minus his signature cowboy boots. He said they were causing too much pain on his heels, so he traded them in for a pair of sneakers. "Well if there are (cancerous) nodes in there they need to come out." He wasn't one to beat around the bush. I told him that although I trusted him fully, I had reservations due to the location of the two nodes behind my carotids. I also told him that I was aware most conventional doctors are against any type of natural treatment but that is the route I wanted to try first, given he didn't see any emergent situation with my carotids being in danger. He told me he was open to me trying what I wanted and that he wasn't worried about my carotids as they are very resilient. When your physician listens to you and is respectful and knowledgeable about your thoughts, it makes all the difference in the world to feel positive going forward. Although he did want me to do a neck CT to check for further involvement and chest CT to check for metastasis before giving me the green light.

In my first consult with Dr. Smith before my thyroidectomy, he asked if I had ever lived near a nuclear site. This was his only conclusion as to how I may have acquired thyroid cancer. Well, I have never lived next to a nuclear site, but I did grow up playing and working in my uncle's orchards being exposed to numerous pesticides. I've had countless dental x-rays since I was five years old never having my neck covered until recently. I've had mammograms and exposure during other imaging. I worked in a fruit shed after high school, again, being exposed to numerous toxic pesticides. I grew up with a mouth full of amalgam fillings that contained mercury, which I did have removed a few years before my cancer. I was exposed to constant second-hand cigarette smoke for my first eighteen years of life. I ran a CT scanner at work for several years prior to being diagnosed. I was raised on mainly a meat and potatoes diet, never consuming the types of vegetables and other cancer fighting foods that are essential for optimal health. All this, along with certain stressors in my past that I now realize I should have taken control over. Stress is a major detriment to our health. So, it is hard to pinpoint when or how I actually acquired thyroid cancer or how anyone acquires any type of cancer.

This has no bearing on my current situation as I have no control to change my past, but I will change my future. I would rather give my body the healthy things it needs to fight this rather than dumping more poison on it hoping to kill it. There are obviously deficiencies in my body, allowing for this recurrence and the original cancerous mass in the first place. Educating yourself and taking responsibility for your own health is the first step in fighting any disease. Do not rely solely on your doctor's advice, as most are trained in conventional medicine only. Nutrition is the key to health. Our bodies are amazing and complex machines that require clean air to keep us oxygenated, clean water to hydrate and keep our entire system functioning, nutrients from fresh organic foods, herbs and spices to nourish our cells and help ward off disease, physical exercise to maintain optimal health on many levels and good mental health, keeping us free of stress to help our immune system. Our body can only give back what we give to it. Cancer is a result of our system responding negatively to an internal or external stressor, a stressor it does not have the proper tools to fight. So, pay close attention to what you give your body, physically, emotionally, mentally and spiritually. Cancer doesn't have to be something to be fearful of. Put yourself in charge of your own destiny.

I have always held the belief that everything in life happens for a reason. Good and bad. Although it is difficult to rationalize why anyone gets cancer or any other life-threatening disease. Maybe I had to endure the hell of this disease and the loss from Kelly to give me the drive to write this book to help other people have a better outcome than I did. It is said that heartbreak is the best motivator, and this is a cathartic project that I hope will let others know they are not alone in their struggles. We are all in this together.

EPILOGUE

This year has been my toughest yet but also my most rewarding. Through heartbreak I have found strength I didn't know I had. I have connected with countless thyroid cancer survivors that have struggled with the same ill effects after thyroidectomy, that share their struggles and have unending support for each other. I have connected with old friends and made new ones that gave me love and support I will never forget. I have been able to enjoy my own existence again after being lost for two years. I have reached out to strangers dealing with all types of cancer and had others reach out to me, sharing knowledge and insight on helping our bodies heal naturally. I have met so many courageous and wonderful people along the way.

I look at this cancer recurrence only as a minor setback, one that has given me the appreciation for optimal health.